THE G.I. SERIES

Billy Yank
The Uniform of the Union Army, 1861–1865

Cover: Union infantrymen in their dark blue woollen four-button sack coats and contrasting sky-blue kersey trousers wear the forage cap, sometimes referred to as the 'bummer's' cap. By mid war, all these items constituted the typical combat kit for Federal troops. The mounted man is a lieutenant colonel of light artillery, so designated by his scarlet-backed shoulder-straps. (Autry Museum of Western Heritage)

An unidentified company grade officer of the First U.S. Cavalry displays the numeral '1' in silver below the officer's hat insignia, in keeping with the directive for cavalry officers set forth in General Orders No [ ] Adjutant General's Office, 24 June 18[ ]. He retains the dark blue woollen trousers that were regulation until 16 December 1861. The epaulets are gold, the sash crimson silk. The gauntlets, although not called for in regulations, were common accessories to cavalrymen, particularly officers.

THE G.I. SERIES

THE ILLUSTRATED HISTORY OF THE AMERICAN SOLDIER, HIS UNIFORM AND HIS EQUIPMENT

Billy Yank

The Uniform of the Union Army, 1861–1865

Michael J. McAfee and
John P. Langellier

Greenhill Books
LONDON

Stackpole Books
PENNSYLVANIA

Greenhill Books

Billy Yank: The Uniform of the Union Army, 1861–1865 first published 1996 by Greenhill Books, Lionel Leventhal Limited, Park House, 1 Russell Gardens, London NW11 9NN
and
Stackpole Books, 5067 Ritter Road, Mechanicsburg, PA 17055, USA.

British Library Cataloguing in Publication Data
McAfee, Michael J.
Billy Yank: The Uniform of the Union Army, 1861–1865. – (G.I.: The Illustrated History of the American Soldier, His Uniform & His Equipment; Vol. 4)
1. United States. Army – Uniforms
I. Title II. Series III. Langellier, John P.
355.1'4'0973
ISBN 1-85367-238-6

Library of Congress Cataloging-in-Publication Data available.

Designed and edited by DAG Publications Ltd
Designed by David Gibbons.
Layout by Anthony A. Evans.
Printed in Hong Kong.

ACKNOWLEDGEMENTS

All black and white illustrations in this vol are property of Michael J. McAfee. Colour im were made possible through the assistanc Michael Moss and David Meschutt, of the V Point Museum, Kevin Mulroy, Autry Museu Western Heritage, and photographer Susan stein. This book is dedicated to the memor Frederick P. Todd.

ABBREVIATIONS

AMWH	Autry Museum of Western Heritag
BL	Bancroft Library, Berkeley, CA
FAM	Frontier Army Museum, Ft. Leaven worth, KS
FDNHS	Fort Davis National Historic Site
FLNHS	Fort Laramie National Historic Site
LBNB	Little Bighorn National Battlefield
LC	Library of Congress
NARS	National Archives Records Service
KSHS	Kansas State Historical Society, Topeka
RBM	Reno Battlefield Museum, Garryow MT
SI	Smithsonian Institution, Museum American History
USAMHI	US Army Military History Institute Carlisle Barracks, PA
UKL	Pennell Collection, Kansas Collections, University of Kansas Libraries, Lawrence
USCM	US Cavalry Museum, Fort Riley, KS
WSM	Wyoming State Museum, Cheyenn

BILLY YANK:
THE UNIFORM OF THE UNION ARMY, 1861–1865

aham Lincoln's victory in the presidential elec-
of 1860 triggered a reaction among seven
thern states. By February 1861 all seven
erted their sovereignty and declared their
arture from the Union. The breakaways then
about the establishment of a provisional gov-
ment, calling themselves the Confederate
es of America. Not long afterwards they
ted to seize federal property, including mili-
posts. Soon, only Fortress Monroe in Virginia,
Pickens in Florida, and Fort Sumter in South
olina continued to fly the U.S. flag. Then, on 12
il 1861 artillery fire shattered the strained
ce as Confederate batteries in Charleston Har-
blasted away against the brick bastion that
od as a symbol of federal authority.

side its casemates, Major Robert Anderson
his command responded with their own bar-
es. The duel proved short lived. By 14 April
lerson and his ninety men were forced to sur-
der Fort Sumter. The American Civil War had
un.

response to these opening salvos, Lincoln
ed upon the governors of loyal states to fur-
some 75,000 volunteers to squash the seces-
ists. This body of men was to serve for three
nths and provide a sizeable reinforcement to
small Regular Army of approximately 16,000
cers and men which Lincoln had at his dis-
al when he came to office. In addition, the
sident gained congressional authority to
and the regulars by one field artillery regi-
nt, another of cavalry, and eight of infantry
imately a ninth was included), as well as
ster into service another forty regiments of
Volunteers comprising some 42,000 fighting
n. On paper all this appeared adequate to the
k at hand, a short conflict being expected.

In reality those who responded early to the call
to arms ultimately proved insufficient in numbers, and at best represented a mixed lot when it
came to trained soldiers led by competent officers. And they rallied to the Union cause in a vari-
ety of outfits that resulted in anything but
uniformity in the early part of the conflict. A
range of colors and cuts made it difficult to
determine which side some of these units
belonged to, and resulted in confusion during
some of the opening engagements. Northern
troops appearing in gray sometimes were mis-
taken for Southern forces.

In other instances the uniforms were gaudy
and impracticable – fine for parades by militia
but not suited to combat. Tall bearskins, coatees
with considerable trim, and outfits which had
been adopted more out of patriotic fervor rather
than practical considerations proliferated. In a
number of instances national origins took precedence over providing a readily identifiable connection with the North. There were Irish, Scots,
Italian, and French units whose members often
hailed from those countries or traced their ancestry to them. In a number of instances they chose
to adopt a dress that reflected these specific
European roots. Then there were those who had
no connection to Europe *per se* but were smitten
by foreign martial fashion – most notably by the
Zouaves, a Franco-Algerian military formation
which roused considerable interest in the United
States not long after the Crimean War. Their uniform was even issued to some African American
units after blacks entered the federal ranks
halfway through the war.

Still other companies and regiments joined in
haste with little concern for their kit. There were
those who arrived for duty in civilian garb, with

only accouterments and weapons to mark them as a military organization.

These men had to be clothed, as ultimately did hundreds of thousands more as the conflict escalated from what many thought would be a short affair to a prolonged, bloody series of engagements over four desperate years. At the start the Confederates held a military advantage, primarily because the Union troops had to go on the offensive and invade the enemy's territory in order, as one historian phrased it, to 'subdue a valorous people zealously fighting for what it considered to be its liberty, its honor, its very existence'. This proved a formidable task. Indeed, during the opening months of the war Southern strategy prevailed. The idea simply was to wait. Union soldiers would have to come to them, and that was just what happened.

In turn, Northern objectives broadened, not only to capture Richmond, but also, as historian T. Harry Williams summarized: 'To smash the army defending the capital, to grasp the line of the Mississippi River, thus splitting the Confederacy into two parts; and after the second objective had been achieved, to seize Chattanooga on the Tennessee River line, thereby securing a base from which to launch an offensive to divide the Confederacy again.'

These ambitious goals proved costly for both sides. The North, even with its industrial superiority, found it not only difficult to clothe its armies, but also to supply them with all the required *matériel* to prosecute the war. Weapons sometimes even had to be procured abroad to arm the growing ranks of the Union. This led to high costs, especially when various agents of the government ended up bidding against one another for foreign ordnance, thereby inflating already high prices.

The feeding of what was to become one of the largest armies ever fielded to that time likewise was a major task. While the canning process had become practical by this period and experiments in the preservation of foodstuffs were being undertaken, the troops still required considerable quantities of 'fresh' food – the term being relative in many instances. Pork, or 'fatback' as it was known, could be old and rancid as could beef rations. These were staples to be eaten with hard bread, a kind of thick cracker also referred to as hard crackers or hardtack. The troops would

soak these items in fat, crush them, or in ot[her] ways attempt to make them more digestibl[e] not more palatable. Coffee was another ma[in] ingredient in the monotonous field fare, wh[ich] also was far from healthy. Many men suffe[red] from lack of proper diet, bad drinking water, [and] similar problems. In fact, many fell ill to a ra[nge] of maladies from dysentery to measles [and] chicken pox. Some died. Many more were ou[t of] action from diseases that took a higher toll t[han] those struck down by the enemy.

Medical care varied greatly, but generally [was] inadequate given the enormous problems c[on-]fronting the medicos and also given the stat[e of] the medical arts of the era. A man might surv[ive] a Rebel round only to die of shock, loss of blo[od,] or complications from surgery, most not[ably] gangrene.

Other problems faced the Yankees as w[ell,] most notably a lack of leadership when it cam[e to] the high command. Lincoln began his search [for] a commander who could stand up to the Conf[ed-]erates, and settled for Major General Georg[e] McClellan as one of many unsuccessful gene[rals] the president placed in charge.

Early the next year activities increased, but [not] under McClellan. Instead, the action shifted [to] the West where, in January, Brigadier Gen[eral] George Thomas gained one of the first signific[ant] federal victories over the South at Mill Spri[ngs,] Kentucky. During the following month, anot[her] Yankee rising star in the western theater, Ulys[ses] S. Grant, also handed the Rebels a defeat by c[ap-]turing Fort Henry on the Tennessee and F[ort] Donelson on the Cumberland. The determi[ned] Grant repeated his success, although only a[fter] reversing the initial Confederate onslaught [at] Shiloh, Tennessee, in April.

April likewise saw McClellan finally move [his] army from Washington to Yorktown, Virgini[a, a] proposed springboard for a drive to Richmon[d. A] number of engagements followed, with the Ar[my] of North Virginia, under Robert E. Lee, fin[ally] sending McClellan and his Army of the Potom[ac] northward by water. The Second Battle of [Bull] Run and Antietam were the unfortunate resu[lts,] with Lee emerging as victor in both cases. [Lee] ended the year by besting Major Gene[ral] Ambrose Burnside at Fredericksburg, Virginia[.]

It was the West again that offered the Un[ion] better news by 1863. After a long siege, a de[ter-]

ed Grant captured Vicksburg, thereby open-
the Mississippi River to the Gulf of Mexico.
other Northern general in the West, William
ecrans, emulated Grant by taking Chat-
ooga, only to suffer a reversal at Chicka-
ga.

he South likewise prevailed in May 1863 at
ncellorsville with Lee's 57,000 men against
,000, under Joseph Hooker. On 1 May the
on leader had succeeded in deploying almost
f his army across the Rappahannock near
ncellorsville, Virginia, even as another 25,000
y Yanks were on their way to join the massive
ance. It appeared as if Lincoln had found some-
e who knew how to drive the war into enemy
ritory. That assumption disappeared when
newall Jackson reached the scene with 30,000
nny Rebs, and joined their comrades, another
000 in number, who had already entrenched
mselves and were awaiting Hooker.

ver daring, Jackson combined his forces, and
her than dig in gave the word to take the
ensive. The two sides soon converged with the
ening contact causing confusion for Hooker. In
process he reversed his tactics and went on
defensive, his troops taking up positions
und the town to meet Jackson's onslaught
d in the process 'were surprised, outnum-
red, outflanked, and unsupported'. So the Yan-
es fell back with only limited resistance.

By 3 May the Confederates had pressed the
vantage. Hooker himself was wounded, but
red better than Jackson, who the night before
d been shot when some of his own men took
m for an enemy in the dark and fired upon him.
ckson died days later from complications after
Confederate surgeon amputated.

Nearly two months later it appeared as if the
onfederates might gain another victory when
ee's army, now organized into three equal corps
three divisions each, set course for an invasion
Union territory. At the head of 155,000 men,
ee moved toward the Potomac, crossed, and by
te June two of his corps were nearing Cham-
ersburg, Pennsylvania. The Rebels were
quarely in the Yankees' backyard.

In the process, Lee lost contact with his cav-
lry, thereby being deprived of a valuable source
f intelligence about his adversary, Hooker. In
he meantime Hooker had taken up positions to
lock an attack on Washington, after which he

asked to be relieved of his command. This left his
replacement, George Meade, with the problem of
determining what move the Army of the Potomac
must make next.

On 1 July the enemy dictated Meade's course.
Although neither he nor Lee wanted to give battle that day, circumstances took the situation out
of their hands. Elements of the Union I Corps
approached Gettysburg, Pennsylvania from the
south-east. Throughout 3 July the two sides
engaged furiously, but Gettysburg would prove
to be 'the high-water mark' of the Confederacy,
ending in a confused mass with many dead,
wounded, and captured. Leaving behind nineteen
regimental colors, the Southern survivors
returned to their lines and regrouped under Lee
to return to the South.

Gettysburg and Vicksburg represented key bat-
tles for the North, allowing Lincoln's armies to
consider other strategic options, most notably
Chattanooga, a railroad hub and corridor for the
Yankees to strike deeper into Rebel territory.
Confederate General Braxton Bragg meant to
deprive the Union's commander, William Rosecrans, of this objective. Both sides marched in
September, the South originally being on the
defensive, and met at Chickamauga. As a result,
Rosecrans' troops had fallen back by the end of
the month to Chattanooga where they prepared
for a siege.

Given this state of affairs, Lincoln looked to
another leader to solve Rosecrans' predicament.
He called upon Grant to resume the offensive.
His faith was not misplaced. The cigar-chomping
general launched his troops against Bragg in
November and soon was in pursuit of a fleeing
enemy. It was only a matter of time before the
Confederacy would collapse.

Events of 1864 further contributed to the
Union's momentum, one of the key ingredients
being Grant's promotion to commander of all the
federal forces in both the eastern and western
theaters. Grant now sought to throw his military
might against the opposition in a concerted
effort, sending the Army of the Potomac, the
Army of the James, and the XI Corps against Lee.
Grant's right hand in the West, William Sherman,
was to strike into the interior of the Confederacy
with as deep and lethal a thrust as possible. By
early May 1864 the time to implement this plan
had come.

Sherman, with the tenacity of a bulldog, drove into the South. Although he faced a staunch foe in General Joseph Johnston, he would not yield. Throughout August Sherman's march pressed toward Atlanta, a critical industrial center. By the beginning of September his men took the city. From there he boldly proposed to continue his advance all the way to the Atlantic, living off the land *en route* and destroying everything in his wake. It was total war.

Even as Sherman was bringing the mailed fist to the Confederate interior, his commanding officer, Grant, looked toward Richmond. In May the Army of the Potomac led off. The invading columns would again clash with the Army of Northern Virginia at, for example, the Battle of the Wilderness, and Yellow Tavern where the Confederacy's dashing cavalier, J. E. B. Stuart, was struck down. In the wake of Yellow Tavern, the Army of Northern Virginia's offensive cavalry capabilities had been brought to a shadow of their former effectiveness.

While Sheridan was wreaking havoc on horseback, Grant made a general attack against both the east and west faces of Lee's lines at Spotsylvania, beginning on 10 May. The fighting on the west proved the fiercest, and Grant gradually turned his concentration on the east, Lee's right flank, where the Yankees hoped to envelop the Rebels.

Lee dug in again, and avoided entrapment. As one historian put it, this 'side-slipping process was continued, from position to position, until Lee came out of the defenses of Richmond, his right on the Chickahominy and his left at Cold Harbor ...' Although he had been pushed back to the Confederate capital, Lee skilfully denied Grant success, at the cost of some 25,000 to 30,000 casualties from his army, while Grant had sustained 55,000 to 60,000 dead, wounded, or captured during the bloody campaign. The Northern press began to refer to Grant as a butcher, but this charge did not dissuade him from his unrelenting course to draw Lee into open confrontation.

With that intent Grant withdrew from the vicinity of Richmond on 12 June. He now set his sights on Petersburg, with an attack on the fifteenth, but the outcome did not go as planned and a siege of Petersburg ensued.

Lee wanted to derail the Union efforts. To this end he once more decided to make a run at Wash-ington in the belief that Grant would have transfer forces to the north as a precau against the Southern raiders. General Jubal E carried out Lee's plan but with little effect. Gr sent only a token number from his army, w Lincoln recommended that a concerted effor made to crush Early. Responding to the pr dent, Grant unleashed Sheridan, whose supe force engaged and defeated Early in Septem and October at Winchester, Fisher's Hill, Cedar Creek respectively.

Early withdrew even as Grant continued press Petersburg, and Sherman kept driving towards Savannah, Georgia, which fell in December. Sherman then moved on toward Army of the Potomac, all the while destroy enemy crops, communications, and ot resources that sustained the Southern war eff Then, in January 1865, he swung north. Ac tional Union troops left Tennessee to join Gr Sheridan pulled out of the Shenandoah with ther reinforcements for the final push to top the Confederacy.

With superior numbers in place and havin number of veteran Billy Yanks in the ranks, Union at last was in a position to force Lee fr Petersburg and Richmond. Lee's reserves be exhausted, on 9 April 1865 he had no choice to surrender his army at Appomattox. The t had come to bind up old wounds, and 'with m ice toward none,' for a nation which had b torn asunder by civil war to reunite.

FOR FURTHER READING

Boatner, Mark III. *The Civil War Dictionary.* N York, David McCay Company, Inc., 1959

Delano, Marfé Ferguson, and Mallen, Barbara *Echoes of Glory: Arms and Equipment of Union.* Alexandria, Va, Time-Life Books, 19$

Schuyler, Hartley and Graham. *Illustrated Cata of Civil War Military Goods, Union Weapo Uniform Accessories and Other Equipme* New York, Dover Publications, Inc., 1985

Todd, Frederick P. *American Military Equip 1851–1872.* 3 vols. Providence, RI, and W brook, Ct, Company of Military Historia 1974–8.

Wiley, Bell I. (ed.). *The Image of War 1861–18* 5 vols. Gettysburg, The National Histor Society, 1981

ve: When the Civil War began in 1861 the regulation
sers were of dark blue wool, although later that year
ral orders changed the color to sky-blue for officers
enlisted men alike. In this lithograph the earlier color of
sers is seen, worn by a sergeant of engineers in the
background and two officers on the left of Winfield Scott,
the general commanding the U.S. Army at the outbreak of
the war. Scott wears his custom-designed uniform, a
privilege extended to all general officers. (Autry Museum of
Western Heritage)

Left: Henry Bacon'
Reveille on a Wint
Morning provides
many details abou
uniforms. The 185
pattern overcoat
issued to infantry
other dismounted
troops in the Unio
Army particularly
prominent. This sl
blue wool kersey
garment was one o
the few items
available to federa
soldiers for protec
against inclement
weather. (West Poi
Museum, U.S.
Academy, West Po
New York)

Below: W. Winner's *Union Assault on Confederate Works*
shows both the regulation forage cap and non-regulation
slouch hats worn by these blue-clad troops in their four-
button sack coats, one of the most common of the oute
garments worn by the Yankees during the Civil War. (We
Point Museum)

v: Major General George B. McClellan wears the 1851-
rn general officer's cloak coat with optional cape, the
silk braid on his sleeve indicating rank. Underneath, his dark blue woollen double-breasted frock coat has three
sets of three buttons as a further means to indicate that he
is a major general. (West Point Museum)

Above: Philip Sheridan wears the frock coat of a major general with its black velvet collar and cuffs and shoulder-straps with two silver stars on a black background bordered by gold embroidery. His general officer's gold hat cords fly off to the side revealing their acorn tips. The hat and gauntlets are non-regulation but typical of the numerous items privately purchased by officers and enlisted men alike. (West Point Museum)

...ve: Paul E. Harney's
...ting of cavalry troopers
...ing the distinctive short
...t which bore twelve
...ons down the front and
...h was trimmed in yellow
...ted lace for enlisted men
...ey relax on patrol. The
...er riding by wears his
...son sash around his waist.
...t Point Museum)

...t: A painting by James
...er depicts mounted Union
...ers on Missionary Ridge. A
...pany grade officer (on the
...side) is indicated by his
...e-breasted dark blue
...len frock coat. (West Point
...eum)

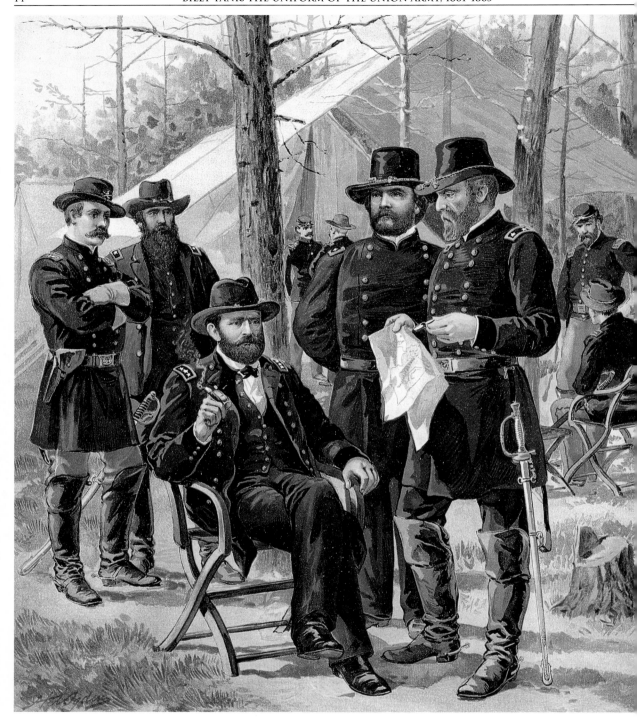

Above: U. S. Grant as a lieutenant general (indicated by three stars on dark blue or black-backed shoulder-straps) looks less soldierly than some of his subordinates, who surround him in this illustration by H. A. Ogden. The practical, no-nonsense look was associated with both G█ and the troops he led in the Western theater of operatio█ As the war continued, function took precedence over fo█ in many ways. (Autry Museum of Western Heritage)

ove: Standing in the center of this composition, wearing
ivilian-style slouch hat, is a major general (indicated by
e nine buttons placed in sets of three on his double-
easted frock coat). He is talking to a company grade
icer of light artillery, distinguished by the unique cap
th scarlet horsetail plume. Most of the remainder of the
icers and enlisted men are wearing the 1858-pattern hat,
ped on the right for officers and mounted troops and on
e left for all other ranks. By 1861, sky-blue trousers with a
arlet, yellow, or dark blue welt were worn by artillery,
cavalry, and infantry officers respectively; plain dark blue
trousers were prescribed for generals and staff officers. All
enlisted men wore sky-blue trousers – plain for privates,
with a ½-inch leg stripe for corporals, and a 1½-inch stripe
for sergeants, all in branch of service colors. The dress
uniforms depicted here, while regulation from 1861 until
the end of 1872, were seldom seen except in Washington,
DC, at least during the Civil War. (Autry Museum of Western
Heritage)

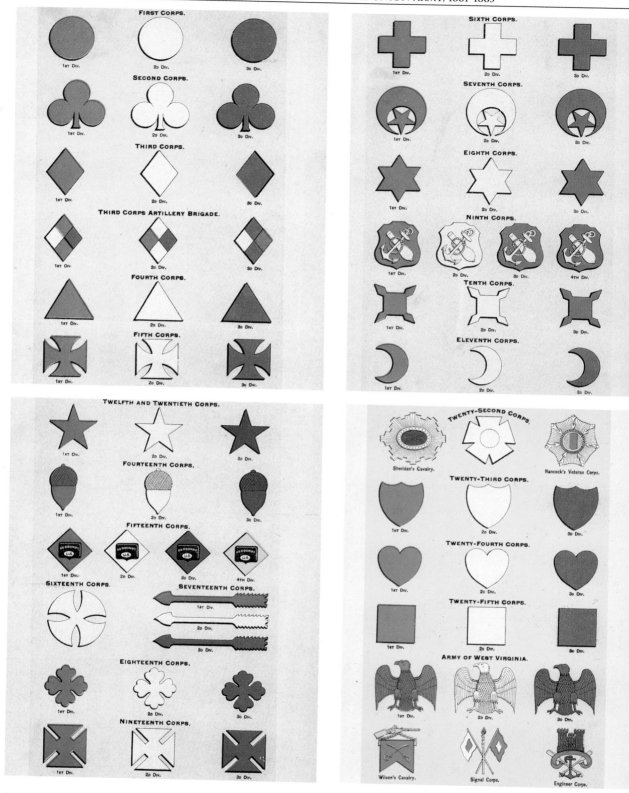

Starting in June 1862, in Philip Kearny's division, Union commanders gradually adopted badges to designate corps and divisions. They were worn on caps, coats, and other garments. Some were mere patches of cloth cut in geometric shapes, other more elaborate designs were made of metal.

By the end of the war numerous types existed and the practice had been more or less regulated into a rational system as seen in these illustrations. (Michael McAfee Collection)

: Although the
n of wearing the
eau de bras
ed from the very
ning of the war,
field grade
rs chose to wear
858-pattern hat
three ostrich
ers, as seen here
by this infantry
r who posed for
ortrait in about
. He is wearing
ark blue woollen
ers with light
welt. The sword
on-regulation
te purchase. Note
he hat is looped
the right side as
eneral Orders
, Adjutant
ral's Office, 26
ary 1861.

The dark blue woollen double-breasted frock coat with
 gilt buttons in each row was regulation for U.S. Army
 grade officers (majors and colonels). It is seen here worn
olonel Erasmus Keyes, Eleventh U.S. Infantry in 1861; his
 blue trousers have the ⅛-inch light blue welt. He is
ing what seems to be the so-called 'French chapeau', a
-dress made available on an optional basis for generals
field grade officers in 1860.

t: In 1861, Brigadier General Scott Negley of the Eighteen
ion of the Pennsylvania Militia had his own ideas as to
 constituted a well-dressed leader of men – they
cted European rather than American fashion.

Left: In the first year of the war the Virginian
Winfield Scott remained loyal to the Union, and
stoically sat for the camera wearing his special
dark blue frock coat of his own design with
gold embroidered oak leaves on the cuffs and
turn-down collar, the same motif being carried
over to his sword belt which has a custom
interlocking circular gilt buckle bearing the
motif 'U.S.' in the center. The wide sash was
buff and the trousers dark blue.

Above: Brigadier General O. M. Mitchel remained more faithful to regulations than Scott and Negley, his blue woollen double-breasted frock coat exhibiting the correctly spaced four pairs of general staff buttons, a total of eight in each row. The plain black velvet cuffs and collar, the red sword belt with three gold embroidered stripes, and the buff silk sash are likewise 'by the book'. He is wearing brigadier general's shoulder-straps with outer edges of gold embroidery around a black center, bearing a single silver star on each strap. He is holding a forage cap with the silver 'U.S.' within a gold embroidered wreath.

Above: Major General J. A. Dix also closely approximate the regulations when it came to his double-breasted fro coat with nine buttons per row grouped in sets of three. has chosen to wear epaulettes rather than shoulder-stra both insignia of rank being correct depending on the or of dress required. His belt, however, is a plain black leat one with a 'U.S.' buckle, neither feature being regulation

w: The distinctive garb for hospital stewards evolved
een 1857 and 1861. In the former year the basic outfit
ly was defined as a single-breasted nine-button frock
with crimson piping around the collar and at each cuff,
matching trousers of dark blue wool. A green half-
ron with yellow borders and a yellow silk thread
roidered caduceus was placed in the center of the
e and these were worn at downward angles above the
w. As of General Orders No. 108, Headquarters of the
Army, 16 December 1861, sky-blue trousers with a
ted 1½-inch crimson stripe down the outer seams were
place the dark blue trousers. A red worsted sash was
ped twice around the waist and tied at the left (as

prescribed for all NCOs from first sergeant or orderly
sergeant and above). This individual is wearing a low-
crowned *chasseur*'s forage cap which bears an officer's-style
small embroidered gold wreath with silver script 'U.S.'
instead of the larger metallic insignia called for by
regulations. A white dress collar is also evident.

Below: The forage cap, four-button sack, and sky-blue
kersey trousers are typical of regulars after December 1861,
when the lighter shade of trousers were re-adopted to
replace dark blue versions issued prior to the outbreak of
the war. The accouterments also are representative for
Union infantrymen.

Right: New York, with the largest population in the United States, accordingly furnished a sizeable number of troops to the Union cause. With many soldiers to clothe, the diversity which existed among New York units typified the lack of uniformity found among the federal forces, particularly early in the war. Private George Miller, Twenty-fifth New York Volunteer Cavalry, wears an outfit no different from that issued to regulars before the war, and which had become widespread for all enlisted men by the time the war ended. The four-button sack coat and the forage cap (nicknamed the 'bummer's cap') are both dark; the kersey trousers are sky-blue.

Left: In 1861, a sergeant of the Second Regiment New York State Militia (later to become the Eighty-second New York Volunteers) stands proudly in an elaborate triple-breasted frock coat which resembled the type worn by the Seventy-first New York, although the broad white stripe on his trousers and the numeral in his hat differentiated the two organisations. Epaulettes with gilt crescent and chevrons, which may be of bullion lace, embellish the coat.

Right: Despite the popular notion that the North always wore blue, many Union units started the war in gray, such as the Seventh New York State Militia. The facings were black on the shoulder loops, cuffs and collar of the fatigue uniform.

bove: The Seventh New York's dress uniform featured
ay trousers, a gray coatee with black trim, and a shako
th a large metal plate surmounted by a tall pompon. Only
e trousers were retained for field use, the remainder of
e parade kit being put aside.

ft: These Seventh New York State Militia NCOs forming a
lor guard exhibit the black lace chevrons worn by
rporals and sergeants in this unit, presumably of worsted
pe either applied directly to the sleeves points down or on
ckings of the same cloth as the uniform jacket.

Above: Officers of the Seventh New York retained the gray
trousers, but instead of a plain black stripe along the outer
seams they had a double row of gold lace over red, in
keeping with the fact that this was an artillery unit. They
also wore the dark blue woollen nine-button single-breasted
frock coat, as Second Lieutenant Tuthill models in this 1861
picture. His plain shoulder-straps with scarlet centers
indicate his rank, and the embroidered cap device his unit
affiliation.

Left: This youthful member of the Blenker's First German Rifles wears a forage cap bear[ing] the bugle device associated with that branc[h.] His sack coat, with adjustable back pleats, h[as] cuffs, collar, and shoulder loops trimmed in green, the traditional color for rifle units.

Below: Even within one regiment, uniformit[y] was not always to be found, as indicated by these soldiers from the Eighth New York Sta[te] Militia, or Washington Grays, who are encamped in July 1861 just prior to the 'Fir[st] Battle of Bull Run'. Most of them are wearin[g] plain, loose fitting gray shirts issued by the state to several regiments as an outer garm[ent] when coats were not available, although the man with the axe has the regimental fatigue jacket with shoulder loops, cuffs, and collar trimmed in black. Note also that the man w[ith] his bayonet fixed has full marching gear in place including a haversack, tin cup, and a blanket roll over his right shoulder which b[oth] Union and Confederate troops often favore[d] over backpacks or knapsacks.

Right: Although blanket rolls migh[t] have been more practical, hard-fra[me] European-style backpacks were iss[ued] to many units, including the Nint[h] New York State Mi[litia.] Dark blue trousers and a matching ja[cket] trimmed in red an[d a] dark blue forage c[ap] with gilt braid wer[e] the standard fatig[ue] outfit; the overco[at] draped on the cha[ir] of dark blue with [red] cuff tabs and a red[-] lined cape. This member of the Ni[nth] is a corporal as indicated by his re[d] worsted chevrons [of] two stripes worn points down.

eft: The insignia
e forage cap of
ergeant of the
eenth New York
Militia, Company
ves an indication
he was not a
ber of the
th New York.
tionally, the
nth wore black leg
es on their
sers while this
ber of the
eenth does not.

left: The City of
klyn furnished
ourteenth New
State Militia
r converted to the
ty-fourth
nteers) with blue
ets ornamented
ball buttons and
trim, together with
vests, caps, and
sers. Sky-blue
sers were worn
fatigue duty. This
orm was adopted
860 and drew
n French military
e, but it was a
rid adaptation
er than a copy.

ht: In part because
heir resemblance
Rebel gunners, the
enty-second New
k abandoned their
awberry gray'
form in 1863, in
or of a dark blue
asseur's coat piped
light blue, as worn
this trio from the
iment in about
64.

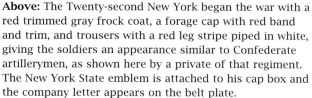

Above: The Twenty-second New York began the war with a red trimmed gray frock coat, a forage cap with red band and trim, and trousers with a red leg stripe piped in white, giving the soldiers an appearance similar to Confederate artillerymen, as shown here by a private of that regiment. The New York State emblem is attached to his cap box and the company letter appears on the belt plate.

Above right: In his state volunteer jacket of dark blue trimmed with bright blue on the shoulder-straps and collar, Private Gabriel Smith, Fifty-sixth New York Volunteer Infantry, is further distinguished by the Roman numeral X, for the unit's other designation, the Tenth Legion. The picture dates from 1861.

Right: A private of the Forty-second New York Voluntee[r] Infantry wearing an 1858-pattern infantry frock with li[ght] blue trim on collar and cuffs and sky-blue kersey trous[ers.] The only features distinguishing this from a regular ar[my] uniform are the brass numerals of his regiment on eac[h] side of the collar, and a bugle device which is smaller t[han] the 1858-pattern adopted for the regular army hat, and – interestingly – is very similar to the pattern adopted in 1872 by the U.S. Army for infantry troops. Additionall[y his] forage cap is the *chasseur* style rather than the floppy[.] 'bummer's.'

Below: White crossed belts formed another part of the Seventy-first New York's outfit as did chevrons of light blue for NCOs – seen on the sleeve of the corporal on the left of the photograph. The officer, a second lieutenant, has no welt let into the seams of his trousers, unlike the enlisted men who appear in this group portrait. The lieutenant is wearing a company grade nine-button frock coat, and h forage cap, which rests on a knapsack on the right of th picture, has an embroidered wreath with the numerals in the center, whereas the other ranks have metal nume on their caps.

ve: This private of the Seventy-first New York State
ia wears the dark blue jacket with light or medium blue
lder-straps and dark blue forage cap. In 1861 sky-blue
sers were provided, with a welt of dark blue let into the
s for enlisted men.

ve right: The 143rd New York Volunteer Infantry had
rian rifled muskets in .54 or .55 caliber, with sword

bayonets. Sergeant Austin Race of this regiment has the
'SNY' (State of New York) oval brass belt plate and the dark
blue jacket with eight New York buttons and standing collar
prescribed by a uniform board in that state in April 1861.
This photograph was taken in the following year. Note the
exterior pockets – a practical detail although against
military fashion of the time.

Left: Cradling his
Sharps Rifle, a priv[ate]
of Company 'A', 15th
New York Voluntee[r]
Infantry, known as
'Bowen's Independe[nt]
Rifles', has slung h[is]
canteen, which in t[his]
case probably was [of]
the type covered in
blue cloth. The trim [on]
his frock coat and
leg stripe possibly [were]
green.

Opposite page, lef[t]
mid war the state o[f]
New York had ado[pted]
a 'polka-skirted'
uniform for its
militiamen, a style [that]
had been in vogue
some New York un[its]
previously. A priva[te of]
the Twenty-ninth
Regiment, National
Guard in 1864 is
wearing the new da[rk]
blue jacket with wh[ite]
piping. His cap po[m-pom]
is red, white, and b[lue].

Opposite page, rig[ht]
In 1862 and 1863 [the]
Thirty-seventh
Regiment New Yor[k]
National Guard
graduated from
wearing the U.S. A[rmy]
frock coat and fora[ge]
cap for infantry to [the]
1861 State of New
York's plain dark b[lue]
fatigue jacket with [sky-]
blue trousers, and
in 1864, to yet a th[ird]
outfit, consisting o[f a]
dark blue jacket an[d]
forage cap, both
trimmed in red, an[d]
sky-blue trousers v[ith]
a red welt. The nu[mber]
'37' appeared on t[he]
cap and breast pla[te,]
the cartridge box, [on]
the shoulder-belt, [and]
the company letter [on]
the waist-belt plate

osite page, left: From
to 1861 the Fourth
lion of Rifles of the
achusetts Militia,
ugh coming from a
that had a
lutionary War history,
ewed the tricorn worn
me New England units
vor of a gray forage
with red pompon and
ace trim. The coat was
with red trim and red
sian' knots. Chevrons
ICOs likewise were red
own here by Sergeant
rney Wales' coat. Gray
sers with a red welt
pleted the outfit, and
ongarm was a M1841
(Windsor) fitted with a
r bayonet.

osite page, right:
tenant Augustus
pson of the Fourth
lion of Rifles,
achusetts Volunteer
ia appears in the 1860
861 officer's uniform of
unit (which became the
eenth Volunteer
htry Regiment). The
ers on his cap are red
the band and the
s. The coat appears to
darker shade of gray
the trousers; it may
been blue. The bugle
is hip reflects the light
htry nature of the
hent, which used
es rather than drums
ignalling orders.

t: Captain William
mpson, who command-
company of the Forty-
I New York Volunteer
htry, wears a short
et with nine buttons
er than a company
e officer's frock coat.
dark blue vest and
sers give a monotone
ct. The black campaign
has officer's gold and
k cords but no other
gnia.

Above: Chaplains, like Edward Lord, 110th New York Volunteers, seen here in 1862, improvised their uniform because they were not obliged to follow the requirements set forth in General Orders No. 102, Adjutant General's Office, 25 November 1861, which stated: 'The uniforms for chaplains of the army will be plain frock coat with standing collar, and one row of nine black buttons; plain black pantaloons; black felt hat, or army forage cap without ornament.' Bible in hand, Lord has added a medical or pay department officer's sword to the basic uniform which, while it conforms to General Orders No. 102, has the addition of a general staff captain's shoulder-straps – a rough equivalent of his rank (chaplains were to receive the pay and allowances of a cavalry captain) – and a sash of an indeterminate color.

Above: A typical embroidered Arms of the United States side-piece for the 1858-pattern officer's hat is evident in this photograph of Colonel Lewis Campbell, Sixty-ninth (Volunteer Infantry, taken in about 1861.

Right: Appearing very much in the garb of a regular, Surgeon Yorick Hurd, Forty-eighth Massachusetts Volunt Infantry, only differs from his U.S. Army counterparts in that the buttons bear the state seal and the cap device i silver embroidered script 'M.S.' rather than a 'U.S.'. The sword is the M1840 Medical Department's edged weapor

Left: Captain Orlando Nims, who commanded a battery named after him, and which was raised as part of the st? of Massachusetts's contribution to the Union, holds a fo? cap with sloping visor popularly known today as the 'McDowell' pattern, so called because it was favored by Major General Irvin McDowell. For some reason he is shouldering a trumpet for this portrait. It was probably ? 'prop', much loved by photographers of the time, but wh? can give rise to erroneous assumptions about accouter-ments and uniforms. His epaulettes are of the type favo? by the militia and volunteers, rather than regular army pattern.

Above: Colonel T. J. Turner, who commanded the Fiftee? Illinois Infantry, seems to have buttons from that state ? his double-breasted field grade frock coat. The shoulder straps probably have a light blue center and bear a spre? eagle to indicate his rank. His McDowell-type forage cap bears an embroidered trumpet of the type worn by offic? of the Mounted Rifles, a U.S. Army regiment established during the Mexican War and redesignated the Third U.S. Cavalry in 1863.

ove: The sloping visor version of the forage cap, often ·rred to as the 'McDowell' pattern, is held by at least ·e of the officers of the Twentieth Massachusetts ·unteer Infantry's regimental staff, in 1861. The spread ·les of the regiment's colonel are evident in the center of ·shoulder-straps (seated man with hand on the table).

·ow: Officers of the First Connecticut Artillery at ·ktown, Virginia, in 1862, all wear nine-button single-

breasted company grade frock coats and scarlet-backed shoulder-straps, with the exception of the man who appears third from the left, who has chosen what appears to be a long sack coat or jacket with five buttons. Forage caps and civilian-style slouch hats are evident, as are two oil cloth covers for forage caps on the young man standing in the rear center, and the standing officer second from the left.

site page: Seated for a portrait in 1862, Captain
el Doten, Twenty-ninth Massachusetts Volunteer
try, has obtained large-sized shoulder-straps with
e bars at each end to display his rank. His tall forage

cap has a gold embroidered infantry bugle device with a
silver embroidered '29.' The coat and trousers are of dark
blue wool. The sword knot hanging from his M1850 foot
officer's sword is gold bullion.

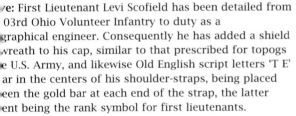

ve: First Lieutenant Levi Scofield has been detailed from
03rd Ohio Volunteer Infantry to duty as a
graphical engineer. Consequently he has added a shield
wreath to his cap, similar to that prescribed for topogs
e U.S. Army, and likewise Old English script letters 'T E'
ar in the centers of his shoulder-straps, being placed
een the gold bar at each end of the strap, the latter
ent being the rank symbol for first lieutenants.

Above: Captain Samuel Walden of the Thirty-third New
Jersey Volunteer Infantry ('2nd Zouaves') is wearing a
standard blue nine-button company grade frock coat and an
embroidered wreath with the regimental numeral on his
cap, which also has additional blue and red trim in keeping
with those worn by the enlisted men.

Above: Captain Lewis Fassett, Sixty-fourth New York Volunteer Infantry, has opted to replace the long frock coat – often worn by officers – by a jacket that reaches slightly below the belt. The buckle on his saber belt probably bears the letters 'N.Y.' in a wreath.

Above: The U.S. Military Academy summer full dress consisted of coatee of cadet gray with ball buttons and black silk cord trim, with white duck trousers and the 1 pattern black cap with leather top. West Pointers anxiou awaited the day that they could put aside this uniform one of a commissioned officer.

: In 1861, this private of the Second
ont Infantry turns out in gray 'doeskin'
vith buttons bearing the state seal, and
ers of the same material. They were
factured by Merrill & Co., of Reading,
ont. The cap was also gray, and all three
were piped in blue cord. As it turned out,
olor tended toward brown rather than

Left: A plain dark blue frock coat and dark blue
trousers, with a 'furlough cap' that bore the
embroidered letters 'U.S.M.A.' in a wreath, were
authorized for cadets at West Point when they
were on leave. It is possible that some
graduates converted this uniform after they
had graduated and received their commissions,
the pattern of the frock coat being of the type
worn by regular army company grade officers.

Left: The Fourth Wisconsin Infantry began war with a gray cap, trousers, and jacket, t latter item being trimmed in black on the shoulder loops and cuff flashes. Most of t regiments from this state followed a simila course, during the first year of the conflict least.

Opposite page: Inspired by the Seventh Ne York black-trimmed uniforms of gray cloth black-and-white epaulettes and a black cap surmounted by a white pompon, was the d kit for the Second Regiment of Massachuse Volunteer Militia, when the war began in 1

Left: These soldi Tenth Massachus Volunteer Infantr hold the 1853 En rifle. Imported fr England, some 5(were purchased between 1861 (w this picture was and the end of 1 The four-button coat prevails as c 'mud-colored' slo hats (so describe the regimental history).

Above: In this 1861 picture Private Minor Milliman, Company 'E', Thirty-ninth Illinois Volunteer Infantry, has added a sash and sword to set off his blue cap, trousers, and jacket, the first two items not forming part of the issue, although his U.S.-converted musket was.

Above: As indicated by their name, the Philadelphia Gr[e]y Reserves had a fatigue uniform in that color, with black cuffs and flashes on the collar, seen here worn by a pri[vate] of that unit in 1861.

Another
delphia unit of
, the
walader's Grays,'
pany of the First
ment Pennsylvania
ery, wore the tall
shako which
s to have a black
pon. The trim on
uniform is
ably black with
laced overlays.
ough this man is a
te, the shoulder
s are of the
ern issued to
s in the U.S. Army
nning in the
0s.

Above: Another example of the dandy dress favored by militiamen at the outbreak of the Civil War is evident in this picture of a member of the two-company First Corps of Cadets, Boston, 1861. This man, in his red-trimmed gray uniform and ungainly chapeau, belonged to the First Company.

Above right: Connecticut's Revolutionary War heritage is reflected by a private of the Putnam Phalanx, a quasi-military unit formed in 1858 (photographed in 1861). A black cocked hat with gilt trim and red over black feathers tops off a blue coat with buff facings, buff waistcoat, black breeches, and gilt buttons and epaulettes. A forage cap,

similar to the U.S. Army's 1839-pattern, is on the table ne to this anachronistic warrior who probably never left the parade ground, at least in this kit, to fight against the Confederacy.

Opposite page: In stark contrast to such pomp, an unidentified infantry volunteer from Maine exhibits a no-nonsense Yankee outfit, which may be of gray cloth, this shade being adopted for the first six regiments raised by the state for the war. The brass belt plate, although reversed in the original image, bears the common 'V.M.M.' (Volunteer Militia Maine)

osite page, left:
company of the
Massachusetts
nteer Militia had its
distinctive uniform
n the Civil War
ted. Depicted here
private of that
ment in about 1861.
gray cloth triple-
sted coat and gray
sers are probably
med in black or
both colors
stering about the
e in photographs of
period.

osite page, right:
ee enormous light
e worsted stripes
n points down on
h sleeve above the
ow mark Charles
kery as a sergeant.
was appointed to
rank in the Second
w Hampshire
unteer Infantry on
May 1862, by which
e he seems to have
andoned the gray
h red trimmed
atee and gray
users in which the
giment entered
eral service.

ght: Colonel Ambrose
rnside, a tailor in
ilian life who later
se to be major
neral of volunteers,
signed the First
ode Island Detached
ilitia's uniform, seen
re worn by a private
that unit. The
immed hat was
milar to the U.S.
rmy's 1858-pattern
d was looped up on
e left side. A loose
ue blouse or shirt of
erino or heavy flannel
d gray trousers
onstituted the simple
ut effective outfit.

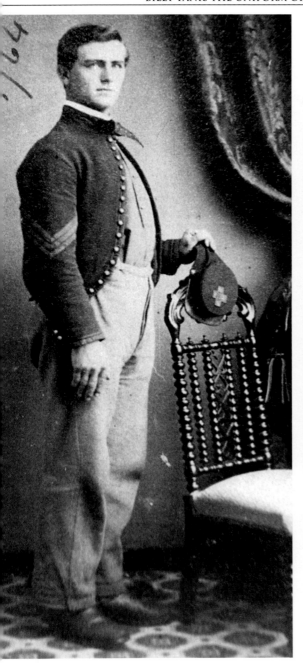

osite page: The Forty-second Pennsylvania Volunteer ntry (also referred to variously as the Thirteenth ment Pennsylvania Reserves, the First Rifle Regiment, Kanes Rifles) gained yet another name, 'Bucktails', use of the deer tail or deer hide badge which the unit e on its caps. This sergeant, as indicated by his worsted rons on the sleeve of a coat which appears to be little e than a civilian sack with military buttons and insignia d, is wearing blue trousers with dark blue worsted 1½- leg stripes. He has a blue V Corps Third Division badge ne front of his bummer's cap.

ve: Beginning in the summer of 1863, with the Third ion of III Corps, cloth or metallic devices gradually

began to be adopted to distinguish major units from one another. For example, Sergeant Michael Lawn of the Ninety- fifth Pennsylvania Volunteer Infantry ('Gosline's Zouaves') displays his VI Corps badge (a Greek Cross) on the top of his forage cap.

Above: In late summer 1862 the 149th and 150th Regiments of Pennsylvania Volunteers were created and likewise placed deer tails in their caps, although the men of the old Thirteenth reacted by calling the newcomers 'Bogus Bucktails'. Both units would have the chance to show their valor and earn the nickname at such engagements as Gettysburg. This private is probably from the 150th PV.

Above: Ethnic and national origins were sometimes evident in certain units. This sergeant of the Seventy-ninth New York State Militia wears his glengarry at a rakish angle in emulation of Highland fashion inspired by 'the old gallant 42nd Scots', according to a November 1858 article describing the unit when consideration was being given to its formation in that year. The jackets were blue with red facings; the men often came from Scotland or were of Scottish ancestry.

Above right: There is no doubt about the origins of the outfit worn by the Thirty-ninth Volunteer Infantry; the unit was known among other names as the 'Garibaldi Guard'.

The Italian *Bersagliere* hat of the regiment's colonel, Frederick G. d'Utassy, and his surname tell the story. The coat for officers was dark blue with gold frogging on the breast and gold lace on the sleeves. The men had red tri on their coats.

Opposite page: The Eighty-eighth New York Volunteers formed part of the 'Irish Brigade', where they were know as the Fifth Regiment, or by their nickname, 'Meaher's C This first sergeant, with the chevrons of that rank prominently displayed, holds the regiment's banner with yellow Irish harp.

site page: Other militiamen preferred
h martial attire, even if slightly outdated,
en here with these two men from an
ntified San Francisco unit of about 1861,
their tail coats, sometimes known as
hammer' or 'swallowtails'. The cap with
pompon is based on a pre-1860 French

t: Colonel Philippe Regis Denis de Keredern
robriand, true to his French origins,
nanded 'La Garde Lafayette', six companies
hich had a French-style uniform, including
y-blue overcoat lined and trimmed in red,
l forage cap with blue band, and red
sers. But not only those of French heritage
enamored of Gallic martial attire.

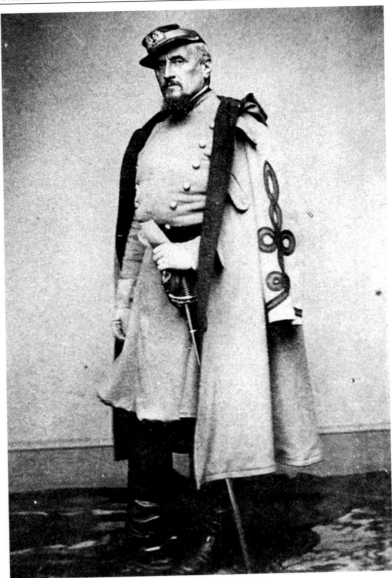

w: In the 1830s the French Zouaves were
ned from a tribe of Berber warriors known
ouaoua. In time these troops in their
nctly North African dress achieved
siderable fame, and gave rise to imitators in
United States. Various militia units adapted
Zouave kit in many ways, the most common
ng a short jacket with lace loosely based on
tombeau, or twining lace which formed the
and cloverleaf on either side of the outer
nent worn by the French Army Zouaves
irailleurs Algériéns (Turcos). Among the
ators were the Duryee's Zouaves (Fifth New
k Volunteer Infantry) seen here at Fort
nroe, Virginia, in 1861.

site page, top: Company 'A'
Eighth Regiment of
chusetts Volunteer Infantry,
n as the 'Salem Zouaves'
ed the gray overcoat issued
e state, but wore a blue
t, vest, and baggy trousers
ed in red. The company wore
rage caps, but three of the
rs, standing in front, have
ed a pseudo fez. The men had
detailed to serve as a guard
S.S. *Constitution* when it was
ed prudent to sail her from
polis, Maryland, to New York
r to prevent her capture.

site page, bottom left:
ugh the other ranks of the
y-third New Jersey Volunteer
try adopted zouave dress,
officers, such as First
nant William Lambert,
ased standard frock coats
ere modified to feature
al trim on the cuffs. Officers'
e caps also had braid,
ugh Lambert evidently found
ch hat more to his liking.

site page, bottom right: A
directly adopted French
ent was the *chasseur*
rm, which was actually
ted from France to be issued
ch State units as the Eighty-
Pennsylvania Volunteer
try. They are represented here
private in the blue 1860-
rn *Chasseur de Vincennes*
t with yellow worsted
ettes, medium blue baggy
with yellowish gaiters, some
ich were leather and others
, white leggings, and a black
er cap with black cock
ers. The uniform lasted only
March 1862.

: The Fourth Battalion
achusetts Volunteer Militia
England Guards) adopted a
rm after the fashion of the
ch *chasseurs*, with kepi,
rs, and knots on the
ders. The jacket was blue.
utfit was made in the United
s, rather than being imported.

osite page: Three
es worn above the
v points down and
tie bars across the
vere the rank insignia
gimental quarter-
er sergeants. This
ple is shown by D. B.
ing of the Twelfth
Virginia Infantry.
an infantry unit, the
was to be light blue,
he material, if it
ved U.S. Army
ation, was to be silk,
r than worsted which
prescribed for
orals, sergeants, and
ly or first sergeants.

t: The sky-blue kersey
oat adopted for
ed foot troops in
, and which continued
ommon item of issue
ore than a decade,
short cape which was
hed to the single-
ted garment that
ned with five buttons.
ap is of the *chasseur*
for this unidentified
te.

Above: In 1851 the U.S. Army adopted a handsome cloak coat for officers based on the French Army's *capote*. The dark blue overcoat could be worn with or without cape. Black silk braid galloons indicated rank, as in the case of Dewitt Baker, Seventy-second Pennsylvania Volunteer Infantry ('Baker's Fire Zouaves'), where five strands grace the cuffs to designate him as the regiment's colonel.

Above right: Captain H. H. Burnett of the Fifth New York Volunteer Infantry wore a coat similar to the 1851-pattern with galloons on each cuff to indicate his rank, but instead of the coat fastening with frogs, gilt buttons were used.

Opposite page: Officers frequently availed themselves of the option of wearing an enlisted overcoat. Lieutenant Albion Dudley, Fifty-eighth Massachusetts Volunteer Infantry, appears to have obtained a standard 1851-pattern enlisted overcoat for mounted troops, which has a pocket added on the right, and a cape lined perhaps in dark blue. The collar of his single-breasted dark blue woollen frock coat shows slightly above the overcoat in this 1864 picture.

Left: Two regiments of sharpshooters were raise 1861. This unidentified private from the Second Regiment U.S. Sharpshoo carries the Colt revolving rifle, and is wearing the distinctive frock coat and cap, both of green cloth, which was the trademark the two units. A black os feather is fastened to the front of his cap. The trou are sky-blue and the trim the coat emerald green. A gray woollen 'seamless' overcoat, also with green trim, is rolled on his Prussian-style knapsack held by straps at the top

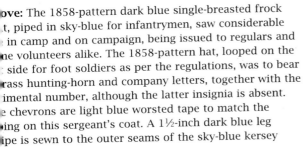

ove: The 1858-pattern dark blue single-breasted frock t, piped in sky-blue for infantrymen, saw considerable in camp and on campaign, being issued to regulars and ne volunteers alike. The 1858-pattern hat, looped on the side for foot soldiers as per the regulations, was to bear rass hunting-horn and company letters, together with the imental number, although the latter insignia is absent. e chevrons are light blue worsted tape to match the ing on this sergeant's coat. A 1½-inch dark blue leg ipe is sewn to the outer seams of the sky-blue kersey

trousers. A black, shoe leather belt adopted for use with the M1855 rifle is likewise evident with its attached frog and sword bayonet in the brass tipped and throated leather scabbard.

Above: The 1858-pattern hat was not as popular as the forage cap, here being worn by a private of the Forty-fourth Massachusetts Volunteer Infantry with his interlocking 'snake' buckle.

Left: Private Louis Troutman, one of more than 180,000 African Americans who joined the Union forces, was a member of the 108th U.S. Colored Volunteers. The 1858-pattern frock coat with light blue piping, sky-blue trousers, and plain forage cap was the standard dress for this unit.

: An unidentified
ant with the
ental standard
 108th U.S.
ed Volunteer
try is wearing the
al belt used by a
-bearer. The light
rim of his
rm coat, the
ons, and the 1½-
worsted leg
 have been hand
.

osite page: Infantry and heavy artillery musicians wore same single-breasted nine-button frock coats as line ps except for a special lace trim which can be seen here his infantry drummer. The young man's coat is too e, so the cuffs have been rolled up, thereby obscuring e of the light blue piping on what otherwise is a esentative image of the 1861–5 era. He also has the 40 musician's sword held by an over-the-shoulder sling its attached circular brass eagle plate.

ve: It is possible that this trooper is a member of pany 'C', First United States Cavalry, given that all the orm elements, including the 1854-pattern mounted

jacket with yellow lace trim and shoulder scales of a private, and the 1858-pattern hat, appear to be of regular army issue. A leather saber knot hangs from the hilt of his M1859 light cavalry saber, and an over-the-shoulder strap supports his black leather saber belt.

Above: Another private, perhaps of the Sixth Cavalry, formed in 1863, appears in the dress uniform set forth in the 1861 regulations, including the mounted troops' sky-blue kersey reinforced trousers. The seam of the reinforcement is particularly noticeable on the inner right leg.

Above: Colonel Louis di Cesnola was commanding the Fourth New York Volunteer Cavalry when he had this picture taken in about 1862. This officer, who was destined to receive the Medal of Honor, is wearing a French-style kepi which bears the crossed sabers and '4'; his double-breasted jacket was of the type favored by field grade officers of mounted units as early as the 1840s. The overcoat appears to be light blue with five strands of black braid to indicate rank. The colonel has slung a pelisse over his right shoulder.

Above right: Although the Sixth Pennsylvania Volunteer Cavalry was officially designated the Seventieth Volunteers, the unit's most popular name was 'Rush's Lancers' because of the fact the troops were authorized to carry a 9-foot long lance with an 11-inch triple-edged blade. The commander was Colonel Charles H. Rush, seen here with a patented cavalry cap-hat. This had not only a visor, but flaps on the sides which could be turned to form a brim. Rush is wearing a standard field grade officer's frock coat and h. tied his crimson silk sash on the left side, contrary to U.S Army regulation.

Opposite page: The Fifth Pennsylvania Volunteer Cavalry carried both Colt Army .44 caliber revolvers, as seen here and .36 caliber Whitney Navy revolvers. The black slouch hat bears inverted 1858-pattern U.S. cavalry and dragoon brass sabers insignia with the regimental numeral above and company letter below as well as a 'P' and a 'V' in brat for Pennsylvania Volunteers. The jacket is patterned afte the U.S. Army model, but it appears that the lace on the collar is in single rather than double rows.

Above: Louis Fagan was a member of the Anderson Troop, an independent company of volunteer cavalry called to arms in October 1861 at Carlisle, Pennsylvania, and named in honor of the commander of Fort Sumter. Eventually an entire regiment was raised and designated the Fifteenth Pennsylvania ('Anderson') Cavalry. Also nicknamed 'Rosy's Ponies', when they were assigned to the Army of Ohio under William S. Rosecrans, the troop remained active until 1863. The patented cavalry cap-hat was a hallmark of the unit, with crossed 1851-pattern dragoon officer's-type metallic saber insignia mounted on the front. The jacket is a variation of the U.S. Army's 1854-pattern with extra seams flanking the front buttons. Brass shoulder scales are another feature.

Above: The Third New Jersey Volunteer Cavalry Regiment (First U.S. Hussars) was formed in 1864, and because of its ornate blue uniform, made by a Newark firm, they were dubbed the 'butterflies'. This uniform was modelled on that of an Austrian hussar unit, the dark blue jacket having a 'profusion of yellow cords across the breast and on the front of the collar an orange colored ground'. Ball buttons were sewn on in three rows. This first sergeant, as indicated by the chevrons with the lozenge above, has crossed saber insignia on his cap with the numeral '3' of the regiment displayed.

t: Bands formed
ntegral part of
y units and had
t latitude in the
of their
orms, such as this
entified musician
e Fourteenth New
State Militia.

Left: The drum major of Fifth New York State Mili sported chevrons similar a sergeant major, but had the additional device of a star in the center. He also wore services stripes abo his cuff flashes, after the fashion of the regulars, a adorned his plastron from triple-breasted coat with officer's epaulettes. He carries a baton and has slung a baldric over his r shoulder as further accessories to his ornate outfit.

Opposite page, top: The band of the Twelfth India Volunteer Infantry wore same quasi-zouave unifo as the infantrymen of th regiment. Many other Department of the Gulf u wore similar uniforms m to look like vested zouav jackets.

Opposite page, bottom l First Lieutenant David Ha of the Sixth Regiment, Ne York Heavy Artillery, wea single galloon on each cu of his jacket as well as shoulder-straps with a si gold bar at each end on a scarlet field to indicate h rank. Gold embroidered crossed cannon insignia sewn to the front of his forage cap with a '6' in th center where the artillery pieces intersect.

Opposite page, bottom right: The brass 'turnkey and bar or staple that he the shoulder scales in pla are evident on the nine-button 1858-pattern froc coat worn by Private Frit Egistrom, Company 'A', F Battalion, Massachusetts Heavy Artillery. So too is leather neck stock which not a popular item amon the rank and file who cal it a 'dog collar' or other derisive terms.

site page, left:
ght artillery cap
scarlet worsted
and matching
tail plume was
d to some regular
and volunteer
artillery units
as seen here in
irca 1865
ait of a private.
acket has a
ly more rounded
and shorter
than the pattern
ed by the U.S.
in 1854.

site page, right:
er light artillery
e appears in a
r pattern jacket
shoulder scales,
he forage cap
ng the 1858-
n crossed
n insignia
ribed for the
hat or cap. The
rcing on the
legs of the
ers is evident.

: Heavy artillery-
such as this
er of the Third
ylvania, in 1864,
wore the single-
ted nine-button
ed frock coat
scarlet piping or
n the collar and
The man's
gear is either an
pattern
ation hat which
een creased fore
ft, or a similar
civilian hat with
arlet cord and
insignia affixed.

Above: During the siege of Charleston, South Carolina, a pair of Union Parrott cannon located in Battery Meade, Morris Island, prepare to go into action in August 1863. Most of the heavy or siege artillerymen are wearing four-button sack coats, one of the most common outer garments by the mid to late war, Also, they are wearing forage caps, with the notable exception of the gunner in the striped shirt. His nondescript hat was perhaps sent from home or purchased from a local sutler as being more suitable for the hot, humid climate.

Below: Company 'I', Tenth Regiment Veteran Reserve C standing at ease, Washington, DC, 1865, the final year of war. By this time the dark blue bummer's cap, four-but sack, and sky-blue kersey trousers were issued extensiv to Union infantry and many other branches, the diverse array of federal uniforms extant at the opening of the conflict now only a memory. The North's industrial capabilities made it possible to achieve this state of uniformity for a large army, reaching at its peak streng upwards of a million men.